Remembering
Arlington

Turner Publishing Company
www.turnerpublishing.com

Remembering Arlington

Library of Congress Control Number: 2010924318

ISBN: 978-1-59652-661-7

Printed in the United States of America

ISBN 978-1-68336-806-9 (pbk.)

CONTENTS

View of Long Bridge from the Virginia side. The bridge planking was removed during the war
to forestall infiltrators and raids. Only a small walkway was left on which to walk—clearly visible
in this image. Long Bridge was the main connection between Alexandria County and the City of
Washington. The first bridge at this site was built in 1809; it was repeatedly damaged and rebuilt. The
parallel bridge was constructed in 1863—shortly before this photograph would have been taken. They
were removed and replaced with the Highway Bridge which opened in 1906. The Alexandria end of
the bridge had the failed development named Jackson City.

ACKNOWLEDGMENTS

This volume, *Remembering Arlington,* is the result of the cooperation and efforts of many individuals, organizations, and corporations. It is with great thanks that we acknowledge the valuable contribution of the following for their generous support:

Alexandria Public Library
Local History/Special Collections

Virginia Room
Arlington County Public Library

The Washingtoniana Division
DC Public Library

Library of Congress

I would like to thank Heather Crocetto, Judith Knudsen, Bonnie Baldwin, and John Stanton at Arlington County Public Library's Virginia Room for their yeoman service and invaluable help; Rita Holtz and Julie Ballin-Patton of the Alexandria Public Library Local History/Special Collections; Karl Van Newkirk, at the Arlington Historical Society; Faye Haskins at the Washingtoniana Division, D.C. Public Library; and Ed Redmond at the Library of Congress.

Donald Alexander Hawkins again provided valuable advice and insight, as did historian extraordinaire Sara Collins; Michael Harrison and Zachary Schrag made insightful suggestions. And thanks to the indefatigable Gerald Swick.

—*Matthew Gilmore*

PREFACE

Historic images of Arlington are a bit more fugitive and widely scattered than those of its neighbor, Washington, D.C. This book brings together around 125 images of Arlington and its vicinity from the collections of the Arlington County Public Library, the Library of Congress, the Local History/Special Collections branch of Alexandria Public Library, and the Washingtoniana Division of the D.C. Public Library.

The varieties of institutional collections tapped indicate an important aspect of the photographic documentary record of Arlington, which has often been viewed from the periphery, from the perspective of its neighbors: Rosslyn in the north of Arlington is adjacent to Georgetown, D.C.; at the western edge of the county is Falls Church. To the south is Alexandria City and to the east the Potomac and the city of Washington. The county has often been defined by its nearness to these neighbors—by what it is *not*—ever since its cession from Fairfax County in 1791. Even then, its name was Alexandria County, not Arlington County.

It became part of the new District of Columbia, the nation's new capital—the one-third portion not derived from Maryland. The new city of Washington was located across the river in the former Maryland portion, and that would become the seat of government. Alexandria City lay at the southernmost end of Arlington (then Alexandria County). With no federal facilities to be located in Arlington, the residents ultimately requested retrocession to Virginia and rejoined the Old Dominion in 1846. With the Civil War, Arlington took on a vital importance in the defenses of the capital. Quickly overrun by Union troops, it was never seriously contested by the Confederacy. Its visual centerpiece—General Robert E. Lee's home, Arlington House—became a potent symbol, along with the many Union dead buried in the Arlington Cemetery.

In 1870, the city of Alexandria separated from the county. The county would be renamed Arlington in 1920. Not part of the nation's capital, now also exclusive of Alexandria city—what was Arlington? Slowly, then with increasing rapidity, it began to serve as the capital's backyard (though facing toward its front—the Mall and Capitol). It became the capital's suburb, in effect replacing those areas adjacent the old city of Washington which had become now more built up. The expansion of rail access and streetcars across the Potomac spurred development. Small-town life sprang up across the county, with the schools, fire stations, and small businesses becoming centers of activity.

Arlington played host to those vices men fall prey to, particularly gambling and alcohol. In 1836, the Arlington end of Long Bridge was developed as "Jackson City," named for then-President Andrew Jackson. It did not prosper but lived on as a low-rent district. The county became a place to play (for its neighbors, particularly), to conduct experiments in flying and agriculture. Finally, in the twentieth century, it became a place to locate those federal facilities which just wouldn't fit into the District—the National Airport and the War Department Offices (the Pentagon).

In addition, Arlington saw the typical development of suburban tract homes (many for government employees working in Washington, D.C.), war housing, and small-scale retail. Postwar Arlington continued to see a population boom, leveling off in the 1960s, and struggled through and led Virginia's efforts to desegregate public education.

Transportation in and through the county was always a prime concern. Commuter rail disappeared, replaced by buses and traffic snarls, only to have rail service reappear as Metro rail, accompanied by elaborate interstates. As the images in the book close, Arlington has become even more tied into the greater suburban Washington, a suburban home to Washingtonians, but conscious of a proud, small-town Virginia heritage.

The goal of this work is to bring together photographs—some familiar and some rarely seen—for a broader audience who will not have seen the whole kaleidoscope of aspects of Arlington: the early rural days, the small Southern towns, the growth of federal government facilities, and the national institutions.

With the exception of cropping where necessary and touching up imperfections that have accrued with the passage of time, no changes to these photographs have been made. The focus and clarity of some images is limited to the technology of the day and the skill of the photographer.

We encourage readers to see Arlington in a new light as they visit, shop, or pass simply through—to reflect on Arlington's heritage and place in the greater national capital region.

An 1861 Civil War image of an octagonal house, the headquarters of General Irwin McDowell, near Arlington House. McDowell would later headquarter at Arlington House.

A Place for Soldiers

(1860s–1899)

The 4th New York Heavy Artillery loading a 24-pound siege gun at Fort Marcy; a letter back home published in the newspaper ran, "Thinking you might wish to hear a little news from the "4th Heavy," I take the liberty of addressing you. Our fort is on an eminence, about half way between the Chain Bridge and Washington; mounts forty guns of various sizes and calibre, ranging from 10-pounder Parrott guns to 8-inch Columbiads, and from 24-pounder Coehorn to 10-inch mortars. It is the strongest fort on the line, with one exception—Fort Lyon, near Alexandria—and with Fort Marcy, a smaller fort about a half mile to the right, and near the bank of the Potomac, has been called the key to Washington." The regiment served in the defenses of Washington until it was sent to the front in 1864. Their experiences were published in a history titled *Heavy Guns and Light* in 1890.

Andrew Russell's photograph of the stables at Arlington House, used for the horses of visiting officers. The architecture of the stables echoed that of the main house, according to the 1934 restoration report: "The fine old stable, across the ravine among the trees to the west, in architectural style and materials, and with classic portico similar to the house." It burned about 1914. The picture dates from a series Russell took in June 1864.

Built in May 1861, Fort Haggerty protected the Aqueduct Bridge, as an auxiliary to Fort Corcoran. With the start of the war, the bridge was converted from canal use to foot traffic. Planks were laid to support a double-track wagon road. This was a very important river crossing—the only one between Chain Bridge miles to the north and Long Bridge to the south. Fort Haggerty was named after Colonel James Haggerty, Sixty-ninth New York State Militia, who died from wounds received at Bull Run. The Sixty-ninth New York State Militia provided one of the detachments garrisoning the fort.

Fort Corcoran, named after another colonel in the Sixty-ninth New York Militia, Michael Corcoran, was the main protection for Aqueduct Bridge. President Abraham Lincoln visited the fort several times. It was located near N. Quinn Street, between Key Boulevard and 18th Street.

Arlington House portico from the south. Many soldiers and visitors had their picture taken on the steps. The house was a kind of talisman for Union troops, being the home of the enemy general Robert E. Lee and having been built as a memorial to President Washington. It was the main Virginia landmark one saw looking to the south and west from Washington. Here in June 1864, soldiers and others pose in front on the steps, along with the groundskeeper.

In 1864, Russell's camera captured a whole crowd of men relaxing on the portico and grounds of Arlington House. This was a very popular spot for group photographs because it was the home of the Confederate commander Robert E. Lee.

Fort Whipple lay almost due south of Fort Corcoran, on land now part of Fort Myer. It has been called "one of the finest field fortifications constructed in the Defenses of Washington" and included emplacements for 43 guns. Fort Whipple was named after Major General Amiel W. Whipple, who died in 1863 from wounds suffered at Chancellorsville. This June 1865 photograph shows black crepe above the door, probably a symbol of mourning for President Abraham Lincoln, who had been assassinated two months earlier.

The band of the 107th U.S. Colored Infantry proudly stand at attention with their instruments at Fort Corcoran, November 1865. All those brass instruments must have made an impressive sound. The 107th was organized in Louisville, Kentucky. It saw action throughout the North Carolina campaign and was mustered out November 1866.

Fort C. F. Smith was one of the ring of forts surrounding the city of Washington. Here Company F of the Second New York Infantry mans the battle works for a publicity photograph. Charles Ferguson Smith, after whom the fort was named, was a Union general who was successful at the Battle of Fort Donelson in February 1862 but soon thereafter died of an injury and dysentery.

An image of the quaint-looking wellhouse at Arlington House. This was a part of the complex of outbuildings which supported life in the big house.

Built in 1892, Curtis (now Carlin) Hall has served Carlin Springs–Glencarlyn at various times as a community center, church, school, library, and nursery school.

Chain Bridge was the other connection of Northern Virginia to the District of Columbia and Maryland. As with Long Bridge, the river often destroyed the bridge—this was the seventh Chain Bridge, built between 1872 and 1874. It was more robust than its predecessors and lasted until 1936. Remarkably, the piers date back to the sixth bridge from the 1850s. It was 1,350 feet long and 20 feet wide, with 15-inch rolled iron floor beams.

Alexandria County did not have its own courthouse until the construction of this impressive building in 1898, shown here shortly after construction. Besides the courtroom there were a jail, meeting rooms, and offices. Albert Goenner was the architect of this and other important structures in Arlington.

The men killed in the explosion of the USS *Maine* in Havana Harbor were originally buried in Cuba. A year later the bodies of 151 of the 253 killed were reinterred at Arlington Cemetery, December 28, 1899. President William McKinley and members of his cabinet attended.

Preceding the current USS *Maine* memorial, this replica anchor, flanked by cannon, was installed in 1899 to commemorate the men killed when the ship exploded in Havana Harbor. On February 15, the anniversary of the disaster, "Maine Day" would be celebrated by placing floral arrangements on the anchor.

BUILDING A NEW IDENTITY

(1900–1930)

In 1900, Congress had set aside a portion of Arlington Cemetery for the burial of Confederate soldiers. The United Daughters of the Confederacy petitioned to erect a memorial to these soldiers, and the Secretary of War, William Howard Taft, agreed in 1906. The cornerstone was laid in 1912, in a ceremony which included Grand Army of the Republic commander-in-chief James A. Tanner (who had lost both legs at the Second Battle of Bull Run) and William Jennings Bryan.

Located at the junction of the railroad and Columbia Pike, Oscar Haring's general store was the first store in Barcroft and one of the first buildings in the area. Folks waiting for the train would shelter here by the stove in bad weather. Oscar's son Eddie started the little local *Barcroft News* newspaper. According to its masthead, the first *Barcroft News* was written, edited, and published in 1903 by O. Edward Haring, the son of Oscar Haring, who ran a general store at Columbia Pike and Four Mile Run (where the Barcroft Shopping Center is a hundred years later). Eddie Haring was then 18 years old. He was "a very bright, likeable fellow and the hero of all the neighborhood belles and the ring leader in all the sports and social events as well," according to Louise Payne's recollection in her article on Barcroft. More recently, we have been told that the actual writer and printer of the paper was Sydney Marye, an uncle of Eddie Haring, who also lived in the neighborhood with his family. Marye's daughter, Adaline Marye Robertson, lived in Barcroft until the late 1990s and, although she was just a babe at the time, she remembers it was a family joke that Sydney insisted on crediting the paper to Haring. (Adaline was mentioned in the 1903 *Barcroft News* as "the baby at the Maryes," and she is still being honorably mentioned in the present-day *Barcroft News!*) The four pages of the paper were only 4 inches wide by 5.75 inches long. The little newspaper served a community of 20 houses, and the masthead proclaimed that it was published in "Barcroft, Va."

A 1903 picture of Charles Knoxville's Sunday Bar. Knoxville's bar on North Moore Street in Rosslyn epitomized the gambling, drinking, and houses of prostitution that Crandal Mackey planned to shut down when he ran for Commonwealth Attorney. Knoxville had run-ins with the law, having been fined five dollars for assault in 1895 and served 90 days in jail in 1896 for selling liquor without a license. This picture was taken during Mackey's campaign.

Temple of Fame at the Arlington mansion, circa 1903. It bore the names of Washington, Lincoln, Grant, and Farragut and eight Union generals--Thomas, Meade, Sedgwick, McPherson, Reynolds, Garfield, Humphreys, Mansfield. Hack drivers, tour guides of the day, told credulous tourists that those generals were buried under each column. The adjacent flower bed had the number of unknown soldiers buried in the cemetery spelled out in plantings. Despite being a noted and popular landmark, it was torn down when the Lee rose garden was recreated in 1966.

Aqueduct Bridge, viewed from the steps made famous in the movie *The Exorcist,* next to the Capital Traction car barn. This bleak, snowy winter view shows a bit of pedestrian traffic and the trolleys on the bridge around 1900. The rural nature of the county is evident in the view beyond. To the far right across the Potomac is the Arlington Brewery (in 1920 it would become the Cherry Smash bottling plant).

Carl Porter competes as a Boy Scout in a fire-starting competition around 1910. This was Boy Scout Troop no. 1. Scouting began in Arlington in 1907.

Rosslyn Station in 1910 shows a crowded urban-suburban commuter transfer station. Looming in the distance across the Potomac is the Georgetown car barn.

Built in 1695, Abingdon was the home of John Parke Custis, son of Martha Custis Washington and the birthplace of Nellie Custis and George Washington Parke Custis. On their father's death just six months later, George Washington brought the children into his family at Mount Vernon. The estate passed out of family hands, and the house ultimately went into sad decline, as shown in this photograph from around 1910. The decrepit structure, on the verge of preservation, burnt to the ground in 1930. The remains, threatened with destruction in the face of expansion of National Airport 70 years later, met with a furor, resulting in their rescue.

The Ballston station looks like that found in any small town across America. Smoot and Warring offered the chance to buy your groceries while you waited or upon your return.

Clarendon Circle pictured here is dominated by the trolley. The circle marked the commercial center of the county well into the twentieth century.

General Bennet H. Young addresses the crowd assembled for the unveiling of the Confederate war dead memorial at Arlington Cemetery, June 4, 1914. Young was commander of the United Confederate Veterans. President Woodrow Wilson is visible to the left. Moses Ezekiel designed the monument, which the United Daughters of the Confederacy paid for and still maintain. Bitter feelings after the war had finally ebbed enough by 1900 for a spot to be officially designated for burial of Confederate dead at Arlington, and installation of the memorial was an attempt at further reconciliation.

Confederate veterans in uniform leave the Confederate Memorial in Arlington Cemetery. The impressive Confederate memorial is rich in symbolism. On top of the 32-foot monument, the larger-than-life figure of a woman represents the South. She holds a laurel wreath toward the south, commemorating the dead soldiers of the Confederacy. She holds a pruning hook on a plow stock, referencing the biblical passage "They shall beat their swords into plow shares and their spears into pruning hooks." She stands on a plinth with 14 shields representing the thirteen Confederate states and Maryland. Minerva, Roman goddess of wisdom and war, is below with figures that represent the fallen South and the military services. Six vignettes depict Southerners of various races.

This Baltimore and Potomac Railroad train station at Glencarlyn, photographed around 1910, was built about 1890. Samuel S. Burdett, a former Missouri congressman and Union commander, developed Glencarlyn as the first residential neighborhood community in the county, platted in 1887. This was on the site of the Carlin Springs resort, which had included two springs, an ice cream parlor, a restaurant, a dance pavilion, and a swimming hole. A new station was built in 1918.

The handsome Arlington Trust Company building at North Moore Street and Lee Highway in Rosslyn was an important landmark. The Arlington Trust Company was organized in 1913 by most of the eminent men of the county and a few Washingtonians, including Fall Church's M. E. Church, W. C. Gloth, John B. Henderson of Washington, and Commonwealth's Attorney Crandal Mackey. The new institution took over the 1908 Arlington National Bank building in Rosslyn, expanding it in 1915 and 1927. In 1977, ATC merged into Financial General Bankshares. The gentlemen pictured here around 1913 are employees C. T. Merchant, Herman L. Bonney, and Bernard Boldin.

Members of the Independent Order of Odd Fellows on the steps of Ballston School. The Odd Fellows (or IOOF) were a fraternal organization offering social and financial support to members. The county played host to several lodges; this is probably Cherrydale no. 42 Lodge, the county's oldest.

Organized fire fighting began in Cherrydale in 1898. Early in the twentieth century, more companies were formed, including the all-black East Arlington Volunteer Fire Company shown here. East Arlington (also known as Queen City) was a tight-knit black community with its roots in the Reconstruction Freedman's Village. In 1941, the area was acquired by the federal government and demolished for construction of the Pentagon complex.

Racing—horse, automobile, and bicycle—was a popular Arlington pastime. The track was located in Jackson City, at the end of the bridge to Washington, D.C. The time recorded here of six minutes and seven seconds betters that of George Fisher (seven and one-quarter minutes) in 1922.

Aerial view of Arlington Cemetery to the west around 1921, dominated by the 5,000-seat Amphitheater. Visible farther west is the mast of the USS *Maine* Memorial.

President Warren G. Harding presided over ceremonies for the burial of the Unknown Soldier at Arlington National Cemetery, November 11, 1921. An enormous crowd of more than 100,000 gathered to salute the war dead. Harding's speech was also broadcast to loudspeakers at Madison Square Garden in New York and Civic Auditorium in San Francisco.

This crowd at the Armistice Day ceremony for the burial of the unknown soldier of the Great War. Over 100,000 people flooded the area. The president was trapped in the traffic jam and only arrived at 11:55 A.M. for the ceremony, which was to start at noon. This was one of the events which prompted the construction of a new Potomac River crossing—Arlington Memorial Bridge.

President Harding's inaugural Armistice Day ceremony at the Tomb of the Unknown Soldier in 1921 began a tradition. He repeated the ceremony in 1922.

The original caption for this photograph from around 1924 reads, "When we had banquets in those days we really had them." This is a huge gathering of at least 500 men for the Cherrydale Fire Department banquet. Starting in 1916, these were grand affairs with addresses from prominent Virginia politicians.

President Calvin Coolidge speaking at Decoration Day (now Memorial Day) ceremonies at Arlington, May 30, 1925. Aged Civil War veterans of the Grand Army of the Republic sit below him. Two thousand people attended, filling the amphitheater. Graves at cemeteries throughout the city were decorated. The speech was broadcast across the nation.

Virginia Hardware Company in Rosslyn, 2016 North Moore Street, opened in 1923. Harry Goldman ran the landmark business for many years. In 1963, it moved to Clarendon at 2915 Wilson Boulevard.

This image from one of National Photo Company's Herbert E. French albums is one of a sequence of images documenting the ceremony of the interment of a soldier at Arlington Cemetery, around 1926.

The observation of the 16th anniversary of the discovery of the North Pole, observed at Admiral Robert E. Peary's grave on April 6, 1925. The eighth anniversary of the United States' entry into the First World War was also observed with a moment of silence. Admiral Luther Gregory, Dr. James Howard Gore, Mrs. Edward Stafford, and Captain E. W. Scott are among those seen here. Gregory and Gore gave the eulogies, and Scott was master of ceremonies.

In 1927, the Arlington County's water system was linked into the Washington Aqueduct. Turning on the water from Dalecarlia Reservoir came with massive celebration—a parade, speeches, barbecue, fireworks, and dancing. The parade began at the Peace Monument just west of the U.S. Capitol, wending its way through Washington, across the Potomac, and all the way to Lyon Village. This float hearkens back to earlier days of wells and water pumps.

Arlington Beach was an amusement park on the Virginia shore of the Potomac just north of the Highway Bridge. It opened May 19, 1923, to a crowd of 7,000, and flourished in the 1920s. Swimming, rides, games, and a merry-go-round were featured, in addition to canoeing. It later added a Ferris wheel and a roller coaster and had dancing and night swimming. General admission was free. It closed in 1929 and was demolished to expand the nearby airport.

Another image from one of National Photo Company's Herbert E. French albums. This is the honor guard at the Tomb of the Unknown Soldier. This 1926 image shows the simple slab on the tomb before the January 1932 installation of the now-familiar, large, marble memorial in the form of a sarcophagus.

The Amphitheater at Arlington National Cemetery, completed in 1921. The GAR's Ivory G. Kimball lobbied for the construction of the new, grander place of assembly. A commission reported in 1909, legislation was passed in 1913, and ground was broken in 1915. This white marble edifice, designed by Carrere and Hastings, replaced the original amphitheater, which was built in 1868.

Two airports existed on the shore of the Potomac: Hoover Airport, which opened in 1926, and Washington Airport, which opened in 1927. Hoover Field was opened by Philadelphian Thomas Mitten who had a contract to fly for the postal service and hoped to foster a new age of passenger flight with flights to the Philadelphia Sesquicentennial International Exposition. The nearby Washington Airport hosted Seaboard Airlines, which flew daily to New York. In 1930, the two fields were combined into Washington-Hoover and a new Art Deco terminal built. Washington–New York Airline, for which the plane in the foreground flew, was established in the late 1920s.

The police department in 1929. From left are Sheriff Howard Fields, Jack Conway, Archie Richardson, Jim East, Hugh Jones, John Burke, Roy Cobean, and Raymond Crack. On February 1, 1940, the Arlington County Police Department was formed, separate from the county sheriff's office, and had a force of nine. Harry L. Woodyard, a deputy sheriff for the county, became the first chief of police.

Originally captioned "Vine Street and Lee Boulevard" intersection, this image will be more familiar as Arlington Boulevard and Lexington Street. The view west of this impressive boulevard is virtually empty of traffic around 1930. Amid controversy, the Lee Highway Association chose the route of the boulevard in 1926, the most southerly of the three options. Lee Intercontinental Highway was supposed to stretch from Washington to San Diego. President Hoover ceremonially turned the first earth at Fort Buffalo in 1931. Five miles were built, then progress stalled. The final connection to Memorial Bridge opened in 1938.

The view south from the intersection of Vine and Lee shows a still-forested rural area of the county.

Washington-Lee opened in 1925 to more than 700 students. Very fondly remembered by its graduates, the entire building has been demolished and replaced with a new facility.

Washington–New York Airline, for which the plane in the foreground flew, was established in the late 1920s. One of their planes and a passenger are seen here at Washington Airfield around 1929.

Multimodalism 1920s-style: early automobiles, trucks, and a couple of horses all at a train stop at Thrifton. Impressive houses sit just above the train stop. In 1920, the streets were being paved to connect the village with Dominion Heights, then farther to nearby Rosslyn. The village slogan "A good place to live" was adopted in 1923.

Preston was one of those houses owned by the expansive Calvert family and was located on the south side of the mouth of Four Mile Run at the Potomac.

Arlington Hall Junior College was a private school for girls, opened in 1927. It was closed in 1942, when the United States government took it over to house the Army's Signal Intelligence Service. Arlington Hall was founded by William Martin, president of Sullins College, Bristol, Virginia. This image gives some idea of the extensive campus, which was an irresistible temptation for a space-hungry federal government. At upper-right in the picture is the colonnaded main hall. To the lower left are the stables and riding area for the equestriennes.

The Arlington Hall school aimed to produce well-rounded young women, with an emphasis on academics, physical education, and the social graces. The Main Hall, in front of which these young ladies pose, opened in 1927 and was completed in 1928.

Families decorating the graves of soldiers at Arlington Cemetery on Decoration Day, May 30, 1929. President Herbert Hoover spoke at services at the cemetery, which was preceded by a parade. Decorations were placed at all cemeteries around Washington, and wreaths were placed on memorials throughout the city.

A rare interior shot of an A&P (Great Atlantic and Pacific Tea Company) store around 1930. The chain, founded in New York by George Huntington Hartford and George Gilman, once was the nation's dominant grocery retailer. This site is now Arlington Hardware at 2920 Columbia Pike.

Frank L. Ball pitching horseshoes around 1930; his friends include Emory Hosmer, Homer Thomas, John Locke Greene, and John C. McCarthy. Gadfly Greene was a fellow lawyer and would serve as county treasurer. Hosmer would serve as a judge on the Arlington Circuit Court. McCarthy was Ball's law partner.

From Washington's Backyard to Suburban Heartland

(1931–1970s)

The youngest victim of this plane crash at Washington-Hoover Airport on November 7, 1931, was 14-year-old Preston Paynter, a McKinley High School student. Pilot Frederick Korte and Lester K. Dennis also perished. The engine on the two-year-old Challenger biplane failed. Here a group of onlookers survey the wreckage.

A quiet, daytime picture of Fort Myer Drive, also known as "Pork Chop Row." This neighborhood in Rosslyn was notorious for gambling, drinking, and other vices.

Impressive 1938 view of the Potomac and the Arlington Memorial Bridge, with nine planes flying in formation. This view shows Rosslyn and Georgetown at the top, and the recently completed Arlington Memorial Bridge below Analostan Island, linking Virginia and the District. Washington's military temporary buildings known as "tempos" are visible at upper-right.

This image shows a plane low on takeoff from Washington-Hoover Airport over the nearby commercial strip. The airfield was hampered by its poor location, divided by a main road, and on low-lying land prone to flooding.

The Georgetown and Alexandria Road intersection with Columbia Pike in what was called South Washington, illustrating the potential for roadway improvements, December 2, 1934. The pike had been constructed in 1808.

Famous image of airplane taking off from Washington-Hoover Airport, passing perilously near to the cars on the road below. In the distance is the Highway Bridge which replaced Long Bridge.

Washington Airport was the original southern airfield, combined with Hoover Field to the north to become Washington-Hoover Airport. This photograph is from around 1935.

Carrie Sutherlin (left) was the president of Arlington Hall Junior College. Frances Jennings (right) was the dean. Photographed around 1937, the two proudly show off some exotic gifts, including several bunches of bananas.

The south entrance of the Main Building at Arlington Hall, around 1930. Several years after it opened, the flowers that bloom in the spring create a bucolic setting.

Buckingham Village garden apartment complex, toward the south. In 1936, Paramount Communities purchased land between North Carlin Springs Road, North Glebe Road, and Lee Boulevard (now Arlington Boulevard). Allie Freed, the chairman of the Committee for Economic Recovery under President Franklin D. Roosevelt, spearheaded the development of Buckingham Village. He aimed to spur economic recovery through privately financed housing developments, supported by financing provided by the Federal Housing Administration. The first units opened in 1937 and the project was mostly complete by 1941. The complex was promoted as a successful example of affordable housing—a New Deal housing-program success and an example for the nation.

The District of Columbia had very stringent milk quality standards, which Arlington dairies that supplied the capital had to meet. Arlington Dairy had a rating of 99.54 out of 100 for raw milk, and above 90 for pasteurized milk in 1939.

Jackson City at the Virginia end of the Long Bridge was also called "South Washington," as seen on the store sign pictured here around 1939. Construction of the Pentagon swept away a variety of stores, industries, and homes, including the African-American neighborhood of Queen City or East Arlington.

A team of mechanics working on restoring a junked car. A whole series of pictures were taken by FSA photographer John Collier at Martin Auto Body in Arlington, May 1942.

An image of the impressive fleet of trucks for refuse collection in Arlington, nine in all. In 1942, the county began residential refuse collection, ending private contracting, but with no provision for commercial establishments.

Arlington took its image (and the reality behind it) seriously. Countywide clean-up campaigns started as early as 1932, spurred by civic associations which had sponsored them locally since the early 1920s. Shown here is part of the effort in the "clean up and paint up" campaign from 1942. The county provided trucks to remove junked automobiles and bulk trash such as tree branches for free.

Dairy production was big business in Arlington. This milk pasteurizer is all sparkling clean for inspection, June 25, 1940. Nelson Reeves was Arlington's last dairy farmer, leaving the business in 1955.

Marcey Brothers ran Arlington County Dairy, from what is now the Cooper-Trent Building on Wilson Boulevard. This image is from the Public Health Department's Rural Health Conservation scrapbook of 1940.

Health Department officials, looking a bit out of place as they inspect dairy cattle in 1942. Arlington helped supply Washington with milk, as part of the capital's milkshed. In the 1930s, the Federal Trade Commission investigated milk supplies and Congress could be counted on to keep a watchful eye on the issue. Congressman Smith of Alexandria called for the investigation of "bootleg" milk sales in the District in 1939. Increases in demand led to price increases and union strife.

A famous image showing an Arlington Health Department inspector inspecting a well in 1942. The Health Department was organized in 1919. From this strikingly rural image one wouldn't guess that the locale was the suburbs of Washington, D.C. This image is from the department scrapbook.

A baker's dozen of students plus one, sitting on the fountain at the south entrance to Arlington Hall's Main Building around 1940. The fountain was a favorite gathering spot for students and faculty alike. The shrubbery has been tamed into sculptured forms.

At Arlington Cantonment, members of Company M, Twelfth Infantry, execute bayonet maneuvers for the camera. Marion Post Wolcott was taking pictures for the Office of War Information.

Some soldiers inspect the new "trackless" tank being demonstrated at Fort Myer, April 21, 1941. This tank was manufactured by the Trackless Tank Corporation of New York and submitted to the Ordnance Department, U.S. Army, for inspection. Preliminary tests indicated that the tank might be adaptable for reconnaissance purposes, possibly replacing scout cars. The tank weighed 10 tons and could reach speeds up to 85 M.P.H. on flat ground.

Besides the trackless tank, another prototype vehicle was put through its paces at Fort Myer, a new Bantam truck. This small, light vehicle was a low-silhouette, narrow-tread, 4-wheel-drive car with no armor protection, designed to carry three men and their weapons. Officially designated the "Truck 1/4-ton 4 x 4," servicemen called them "jeeps."

Kay Dowd marks the flight reservation board at National Airport. Howard Liberman of the Farm Service Administration took this photograph as part of a sequence of women airport and aircraft workers in August 1942. (She may have also moonlighted in the theater—a Kay Dowd was in Ed Wynn's *Boys and Girls Together* at National Theater the previous September.)

The tent colony at Arlington Cantonment at Fort Myer looks rather temporary, if in a military way. In May 1941, these tents were erected to provide accommodations for 268 visiting soldiers of the 12th Infantry. The tents were borrowed from 4-H, and the land was that of the Arlington experimental farm. Nightly rental was 50 cents. The cantonment was later developed into South Post Fort Myer, which disappeared with expansion of Arlington Cemetery in 1960. In its brief existence, it published a newspaper, the *Arlington Cantonment Sentinel* and was the home of the Provost Marshal General School.

Arlington invested in recreation for its children in the 1940s, even though it was segregated. Here youth prepare for a performance of the *Mikado* (or something very similar).

Physical education, including horseback-riding, tennis, archery, shooting, swimming, and golf was part of the educational program of Arlington Hall, all designed to produce well-rounded young women. These students were photographed about 1940.

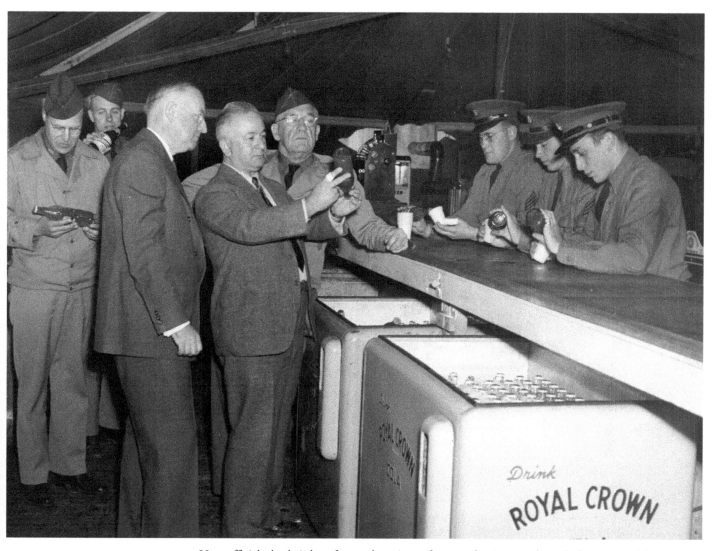

Here officials do their best for our boys in uniform, as they inspect the soda fountain and its products at Arlington Cantonment. This is a posed photograph; the cap is still on the bottle from which the sergeant at the far end of the counter is "pouring" a drink.

The Harrison-Douglas machine shop in South Washington was one of the not-so-attractive facilities torn down for the construction of the Pentagon in 1941. It was located at Columbia Pike and Alexandria-Georgetown Road.

The construction of the Pentagon was a herculean task. The location was ramrodded through by Brigadier General Brehon B. Sommervell, Chief of the Construction Division of the Office of the Quartermaster General. Construction was by the John McShain company, which could honestly boast that they "built Washington"—or at least many of the federal facilities of the 1930s and 1940s.

With the Tomb of the Unknown Soldier being one of the notable sites of Washington, and especially significant in wartime, FSA photographer John Collier posed this photogenic couple there, one in a sequence of images he made in this study in May 1943.

The Pentagon was built in 16 months, on a difficult site. Part of the site was fill, dredged from the Potomac River, part was land snatched from a variety of businesses and residents. Queen City, a small African-American neighborhood, was bulldozed, as were factories and shops. The last remnants of disreputable Jackson City disappeared.

One of the charming members of the Women's Committee poses in a jeep with a WAC and two soldiers around 1942. The Alcova Theater where the war bond program was administered is immediately behind the photographer.

Citizens line up outside the firehouse to vote in the 1944 presidential election, November 7, 1944. This long line is indicative of the predicted record turnout in Arlington (56,784 voters), where a county board member, congressman, and two constitutional amendments were on the ballot. Clear, crisp weather and the contest between four candidates for Congress brought a heavy turnout. Photographer Maria Ealand, niece of Edward Bruce, who headed the Treasury's arts program, worked for the Office of War Information.

Postwar image of agricultural bounty, as a woman selects produce from heaps of tomatoes.

"Downtown" Arlington, that is, Clarendon. It was here that retail shops clustered. Yeatman's Hardware, pictured in the upper right, opened in 1940, and Sears, J. C. Penney, and F. W. Woolworth were on Wilson Boulevard. George M. Yeatman, president of Yeatman's Hardware was a prominent civic leader in Clarendon, as he had been previously in Washington. Here Wilson Boulevard merges with North Hartford and North Highland streets. Today, Clarendon Metro station is located on the site visible at lower-left in this image.

National Airport opened in 1941, replacing the sorely antiquated Washington-Hoover Airport to the north. Here spectators enjoy sitting on the hill overlooking the runways, watching the planes take off and land in 1946.

Postwar years brought prosperity to Arlington and the opportunity for the young to dress up in school pageants. Pictured here are students from Cherrydale school in 1946.

Arlington County Police show off their 14 new patrol cars in 1946.

The paving of Clarendon Circle looks a bit worse for the wear, but Wilson Boulevard downtown is festooned with flags and bunting, presumably for the centennial celebration. Ashton Theater, visible in the middle left of the picture, would have been the site of bond drives during the war.

Arlington County Fire Department was an entirely volunteer system until 1940, when the county shifted to a fully paid department, supplemented by a volunteer force. Here, around 1948, members of the Arlington County volunteer firemen's association play baseball.

Soap box racing was taken very seriously in the 1940s. In 1949, the national competition was witnessed by 40,000 people—148 entries from the United States, Canada, and Panama. Arlington's race here is on a much smaller scale but is appreciated just as much by the spectators.

Postwar years also saw a new emphasis on recreation. Though segregated, a great deal of energy was invested in activities for African-Americans. Here we have a dance—with a mix of emotions evident on the children's faces.

Arlington's courthouse, which by the 1940s was deemed inadequate to the needs of the county, is seen here around 1945, before the construction of two flanking wings.

Funeral of General John J. Pershing at Arlington National Cemetery Amphitheater, July 19, 1948.
He died at Walter Reed Hospital, and his body then lay in state in the Capitol Rotunda. Crowds
numbering 300,000 lined the streets to witness the funeral cortege of the much-respected "Black
Jack" Pershing. Pershing picked his gravesite at Arlington years before, marked now by the simplest of
marble headstones.

An atmospheric image of the old Arlington County Courthouse, built in 1898. Frank L. Ball, longtime Arlington politico, saw its dedication as a 12-year-old boy and its demolition 62 years later. The replacement building was demolished in 1997.

The Hot Shoppe in Rosslyn opened in 1940. Owner J. Willard Marriott said the one shown here, the tenth Hot Shoppe, was probably the most beautiful of all to that time (about 1949). "The Rosslyn Hot Shoppe is where you had to go after dances," according to 1943 Washington-Lee High School graduate Norman Trahan.

A later view of Clarendon Circle, around 1950. Here Clarendon Trust Company (founded in 1921) has reclad and expanded its building, seen at middle right. Across the street to the left is an altered, but still recognizable Masonic Hall.

Colonial Restaurant was a fixture of Arlington life, even fielding a sandlot baseball team. This, in addition to "Steaks - Chops - Chicken - in - the - Nest to carry out." Here in April 1951, firemen put out a fire at the neighboring Washington Screen Company, also a longtime local business.

As fire fighters fight the Screen factory fire, spectators watch. In the distance are the businesses along the Alexandria-Georgetown Road in April 1951.

Progress comes to Parkington. Pictured here in the summer of 1951 is reconfiguration of the roads and parking lot expansion. The large building in the background is the new $6.5 million Hecht's department store, part of the Parkington Shopping Center. This facade would be sheathed almost entirely with glass windows where six-foot-tall letters would spell out messages to drivers speeding by. Sutton's Feed Store is the white frame building at the intersection. Parkington has been replaced with Ballston Commons Mall.

A long, long, long line of cars on their way from Virginia into the District of Columbia at 8:45 A.M., December 7, 1951. This is Lee (now Arlington) Boulevard west of Glebe Road. To the left, out of frame, is Arlington Hall. In March 1951, it was announced that an "electronic brain" would be controlling 12 traffic lights to manage traffic flow from Glebe Road to Arlington Memorial Bridge. It's not clear from this picture whether that could be deemed a success, not if it led to traffic backups like this one.

"A drinking driver needs a policeman for a chaser." Around 1955, three motorcycle policemen stand vigilant to pursue and catch any drunk driver who might cross their path. The Arlington police force came under criticism in the 1950s. A report called for them to "primp up smartly and show a bright face," and to learn jujitsu.

A view north and east over the Rosslyn Hot Shoppe across to Washington's Georgetown and Foggy Bottom. The transfer station in Rosslyn Circle, at the center of the picture, has streetcars waiting to go back to Washington and buses to go into Arlington, as cars stream across Key Bridge. Georgetown's Whitehurst Freeway is visible, elevated between the waterfront industries, around 1955.

Everyone loves a parade! Arlingtonians march in Lee Heights (the water tower is barely visible on the left).

The 18-man Arlington motorcycle police force in 1958, just as vigilant as several years before but with new motorcycles, posed here at Washington-Lee High School. A more populous and heavily trafficked county needed a larger motorcycle police force.

Extremely rare opening of the bascule of Arlington Memorial Bridge for the passage of the Watergate concert barge in 1952. The barge was moored at the Watergate steps above Memorial Bridge for 20 years, from 1945 to 1965, until it became unsafe to use.

The Brown vs. Board of Education ruling, which struck down "separate but equal" schooling nationwide, was not immediately accepted in Virginia. The legislature launched a campaign of "massive resistance," which denied state funds to schools that integrated. This was struck down by the courts in 1959, leading to immediate integration of the schools.

The three-mile bicycle path at Four Mile Run opened September 4, 1967. The $35,000 project ran from North Roosevelt Street to Columbia Pike along the creek. Here a big crowd of cyclists mills around waiting for the opening.

North Moore Street, one block west of Lynn Street, in 1963.

A historical marker in front of this church reads, "Walker Chapel, a small frame country church of the Mount Olivet Circuit, was dedicated at this location on July 18, 1876. It was named in honor of the Walker family who donated the Walker Grave Yard as the site for the church. A new frame church was built nearby in 1903 although the original chapel structure continued in use as a Sunday school until its demolition in 1930. The present building dates from 1959. The earliest recorded burial in the adjacent cemetery was that of David Walker, who died in 1848." The 1903 church had been Arlington's oldest, until its 1959 demolition; the new church opened in 1960.

A view of Arlington Boulevard to the west. This is the long-delayed linkage of the Lee Memorial Boulevard to Arlington Memorial Bridge. The Iwo Jima Motel is visible at right-center (now replaced with a Quality Inn).

Theodore Roosevelt Bridge under construction in April 1964, not long before its opening on June 23. Debated as early as 1948, the bridge was designed as part of a complex web of freeways for the national capital region. Those for the District of Columbia were mostly blocked; Arlington did get Interstate 66, of which this bridge was a part. Routing of the bridge across the southern end of Theodore Roosevelt Island faced fierce opposition. In the foreground are two of the four towers of Arlington Towers (now known as River Place). At the time of construction, this was the world's largest air-conditioned project of its type.

A thin line of military police faces a crowd of protesters numbering over 50,000 on October 21, 1967. The demonstration was supposed to be confined to the north parking lot, some distance away from the Pentagon itself. Eventually the obstacles and defenses were overcome, and 30 protesters actually burst into the Pentagon. Norman Mailer and David Dellinger were among those protesting.

Here is some part of the crowd which faced that spare defensive line of military police on October 21, 1967. The protest began with a rally at the Lincoln Memorial. Here protesters cross Arlington Memorial Bridge to reach the Pentagon. Included in the crowd was Abbie Hoffman, who had plans to use psychic energy to levitate the Pentagon—one of the world's largest buildings!

The county widens Washington Boulevard from Arlington Boulevard to 3rd Street, March 27, 1966.

The memorial to Civil War unknown soldiers was dedicated in September 1866 and contains the remains of more than 2,100 men from many battlefields. This is a merest fraction of the more than 150,000 unknowns buried at 83 national cemeteries across the nation, as reported in 1903. The 1921 dedication of the Tomb of the Unknown Soldier has taken much of the attention from this memorial. Reputedly, this memorial was placed in the Lee family rose garden to spite the family and prevent them from ever enjoying it again. For many years the Temple of Fame lay to the south in the center of the rose garden, but it was removed in 1966.

The house of Vera Koehler, almost hidden by dense vegetation in 1972. Koehler's house and many others were sacrificed for Interstate 66. Koehler was party to a lawsuit to prevent the construction of I-66. Area residents fought a long (and in Arlington, unsuccessful) battle against a massive interstate freeway plan, preferring rapid transit. Arlington ended up with a combination, Interstate 66 and Metro rail, some stations of which were located along I-66.

Thomas Jefferson Junior High School opened in 1938. In 1966, Thomas Jefferson was merged with the all-black Hoffman-Boston Junior High, and a report on school facilities urgently pressed for its expansion or replacement. The current building was built in 1971.

A 1971 image of Ballston showing the Parkington shopping center in the foreground. Parkington opened in November 1951 and featured the Hecht's department store, thirty other stores, and parking for a nickel in any of 2,000 parking spots. Down-at-the-heels after thirty years, Parkington was replaced by Ballston Common Mall in the 1980s, although total refurbishment of Hecht's had to wait until 2006 with its conversion to Macy's. The few tall buildings seen here along Fairfax Drive have since been joined by many others.

Notes on the Photographs

These notes, listed by page number, attempt to include all aspects known of the photographs. Each of the photographs is identified by the page number, a title or description, photographer and collection, archive, and call or box number when applicable. Although every attempt was made to collect all data, in some cases complete data may have been unavailable due to the age and condition of some of the photographs and records.